Sneed B. Collard III

ANIMAL DAZZLERS

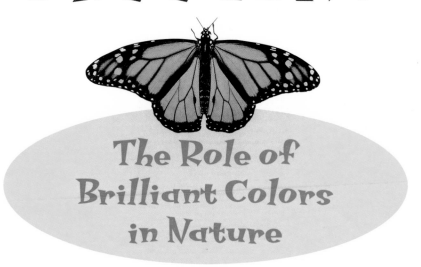

The Role of Brilliant Colors in Nature

A FIRST BOOK

FRANKLIN WATTS * A Division of Grolier Publishing

New York * London * Hong Kong * Sydney * Danbury, Connecticut

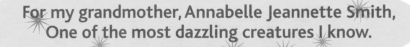

For my grandmother, Annabelle Jeannette Smith,
One of the most dazzling creatures I know.

Photographs ©: James F. Case 39; Sneed B. Collard III 14, 20, 23, 25, 28, 30, 34, 35, 37, 40, 41, 54; Patricia and Michael Fogden 6, 16; JacK Stein Grove 9, 12–13, 51; Richard Herrman 4–5, 42, 45; Richard LaVal 32; William Muñoz 11; Lisa K. Nordquist 64; Photo Researchers, Inc./Steve E. Ross 1, cover (butterfly)Louis Porras 19, 22, 27; Tony Stone Images/Art Wolfe cover (fish); VU/R. Lindhomm cover (flamingo); Norbert Wu 47, 49;

Visit Franklin Watts on the Internet at:
http://publishing.grolier.com

Library of Congress Cataloging-in-Publication Data

Collard, Sneed B.
      Animal dazzlers / Sneed B. Collard III.
         p.   cm. — (A first book)
      Includes bibliographical references and index.
      Summary: Discusses the reasons various animals are the color they
are and explains the science behind colors in the natural world.
      ISBN: 0-531-20362-X (lib. bdg.)   0-531-15918 -3 (pbk)
      1. Animal—Juvenile literature. 2. Color of animals—Juvenile literature.
[1. Color of animals. 2. Animals.] I. Title. II. Series.
      QL49.C67245 1998
      591.47'2—dc21   97-26725
                                                                  CIP
                                                                  AC

Contents

NUDIBRANCHS, ALSO CALLED SEA SLUGS, ARE SOME OF EARTH'S MOST DAZZLING AND LEAST-KNOWN CREATURES.

Wow!

Few of Earth's spectacles dazzle and delight us like the amazing colors of animals. Bright colors serve a variety of important functions in the animal world. Some bright colors serve as warnings. Others help attract mates, and others appear dazzling to us but help *camouflage*, or hide, their owners where they live.

Not all of Earth's animals are brightly or vividly colored, however. Most animal species—including most mammals—are rather plain. This helps them blend in with their surroundings and keeps them from attracting the attention of *predators* or *prey*. The plain colors of most animals, though, make the brightly colored creatures all the more dazzling.

ONE OF THE WORLD'S MOST FAMOUS TROPICAL SPECIES, THE RESPLENDENT QUETZAL DISPLAYS DAZZLING RED, WHITE, AND BLACK MARKINGS WHEN IN FLIGHT.

One

Dazzling Birds
and How Animal Colors Are Made

Of all Earth's dazzling creatures, birds are the most popular with people. Many bird-watchers travel the world hoping to see birds in the wild, especially such colorful ones as the resplendent quetzal (KET-sal).

The quetzal lives only in high mountain areas of southern Mexico and Central America. Perched quietly on a forest tree branch, the quetzal may go unnoticed with its camouflage-green outer feathers. But when the bird flies, it flashes a spectacular display of red, white, and black colors that unleashes a chorus of oohs and aahs from human bird-watchers.

Ancient Aztec civilizations once valued quetzal feathers more highly than gold. Aztec kings and warriors used the feathers to decorate their elaborate ceremonial clothes and uniforms. Today, the quetzal brings a new kind of gold—in the form of tourist dollars—to communities where the bird lives. Monteverde, Costa Rica, for example, is home to a large mountain forest called a *tropical cloud forest*. This forest is the largest nesting place for quetzals in Costa Rica. It attracts up to 50,000 quetzal-watchers each year.

But the bright colors of quetzals and other birds aren't designed to please us. They serve essential functions in the birds' struggles to survive.

Colorful Communicators

Communication is a big part of bird life, and birds communicate in many ways. Many birds sing. Others dance or perform flying acrobatics. Brightly colored birds, however, rely heavily on their dazzling colors to communicate.

Birds communicate mostly with members of their own species. They have many reasons for doing so. Male quetzals perform colorful courtship flights to woo female quetzals. These flights expose the male's flashy red breast, showing females that the male is ready and willing to mate. Similarly, male frigate birds puff out their

8

THE MALE FRIGATE BIRD PUFFS OUT
ITS BALLOON-LIKE THROAT POUCH TO
ATTRACT MATES AND WARN OTHER MALES
TO STAY OUT OF ITS NESTING TERRITORY.

enormous red throat pouches to attract mates and warn
rival males to stay out of their territories. If a rival male
doesn't heed this warning, a fight for a mate or territory
may erupt.

Males with the brightest colors usually rule the roost. They are more successful at defending their territories against other males. They are also more successful in attracting mates. Scientists believe that this is because brighter, bolder colors indicate that a male bird is healthier and, perhaps, a better provider. In an experiment with house finches, females consistently chose the most brightly colored males. These males provided the most food for their mates and young during nesting. The end result was this: females that chose the brightest males produced greater numbers of successful babies than females that selected duller mates.

Fancy Faces

Different bird species and sexes also use colors to tell each other apart. Male yellow-shafted flickers, for example, have black "mustache" streaks on their faces. They attack rival males that have these same mustaches. If a mustache is painted on a female flicker, the male thinks the female is a rival male and will attack her, too.

Adult birds aren't the only ones that benefit from their coloring. Most baby birds are *cryptically* colored, which means they blend in with their nests and environment. This keeps them hidden from the eyes of hungry predators. When mom or dad returns with a meal, however, the

10

babies open their beaks to display bright red or orange mouths. These bright mouths are signs that shout "Feed Me!" They help ensure that the babies get enough food.

Creating Color

One of the amazing things about birds and other animals is how their colors are produced. Colors can be made in several ways. Some are caused by chemicals called *pigments*, which are embedded in the skin, feathers, scales, or fur of an animal. These pigments are like tiny dabs of paint that give off color wherever they are present.

Pigments called *melanins* produce most blacks and browns, and some reds and yellows, in animals. Pigments called *carotenoids* and *pterins* produce bright reds, oranges, and yellows. Pigments are also responsible for some blue and green colors found in animals.

Although animals make, or *synthesize*, certain pigments themselves, they must get others from the food they eat. Many carotenoids are found in fruits and other foods. Flamingos, for instance, get their pink colors from

carotenoids in the small, red crustaceans that they eat. If flamingos stop eating foods with carotenoids, they gradually lose their colors.

Colors also can be created by mixing pigments together. The olive-green colors of many birds are a mixture of blue and yellow pigments. If you look closely at the wings of some butterflies, you'll find a combination of separate brown and yellow scales. Viewed from a distance, these separate brown and yellow colors blend to produce green, much like in an impressionist painting. Pigments, however, aren't the only ways to make color.

A FLAMINGO'S BRIGHT PINK COLORING COMES FROM PIGMENTS IN THE FOODS IT EATS.

THE CROWN OF A BLUE-CROWNED MOTMOT DISPLAYS HOW
COLOR IS PRODUCED FROM THE TYNDALL SCATTERING OF LIGHT.

Separating Sunlight

Sunlight is composed of many different wavelengths of
light. Blended all together, they look white, but if you
separate the wavelengths with a prism, you can see a

rainbow of different colors. Many animals have evolved ways to take advantage of this colorful phenomenon.

The blue, green, and violet colors of many animals come from *Tyndall scattering* of light. Tyndall scattering is produced by tiny particles or structures in skin and feathers. These tiny particles and structures allow longer wavelengths of light—such as reds and yellows—to pass by, but they reflect the shorter blue wavelengths so that other animals can see them.

Blue eyes in humans are caused by Tyndall scattering. Proteins in the eyes scatter blue light and this makes some eyes appear blue when viewed against the black background of the *iris*. Brown eyes also have Tyndall scattering, but in brown eyes, melanin pigments make the eyes appear brown, not blue. Tyndall scattering can be found in many other animals besides us, from damselflies to snakes to birds. The blue color of a motmot's crown is a particularly brilliant example of Tyndall scattering.

Iridescent colors are also produced by altering light. The feathers, scales, and skins of many animals separate, block, and shift sunlight into different wavelengths. These wavelengths are then reflected to produce different colors. Exactly how this happens is complicated, but the effect is a lot like the rainbow of colors you see when you look at a soap bubble in the sunlight.

Hummingbirds display some of the flashiest iridescent colors among birds. Iridescent colors also appear in lizards, snakes, butterflies, beetles, and many other animals. However, there is a big difference between colors produced by pigments and those produced by Tyndall scattering and iridescence. Pigments don't depend on the presence of light to be colorful. The colors in pigments are always there, even if it's too dark to see them. Tyndall scattering and iridescence, on the other hand, only show up when there's light around. That's why if you watch a hummingbird fly from the sunlight to the shade, its brilliant throat and breast feathers suddenly turn dull.

IRIDESCENCE GIVES HUMMINGBIRDS THEIR BRILLIANT COLORING.

two

Dazzling Reptiles and Amphibians

Up close, the skins of most reptiles and amphibians are design masterpieces. Bold stripes, flecks, spots, and diamonds decorate the skins of even plain-looking lizards, snakes, frogs, and toads.

This is no accident. Reptiles and amphibians are favorite foods for birds, mammals, and other reptiles and amphibians. The designs and patterns in the skins of lizards and frogs help camouflage them. These animals blend with the rocks, leaves, or tree bark around them.

Some reptiles and amphibians, however, sport such bright, splashy colors that even the most near-sighted predator couldn't miss them. Among the most fascinating of these show-offs are those whose colors warn predators to stay away.

Hazardous Hues

Biologists have a special name for warning colors. They are called *aposematic* (A-po-seh-MA-tik) colors. Aposematic colors are especially popular among some venomous snakes. The highly venomous coral snake has vivid red, yellow, and black rings that send the message: "I'm venomous. If you try to attack me, you may end up dead!" This message comes through loud and clear. In one experiment, biologists showed that birds attacked

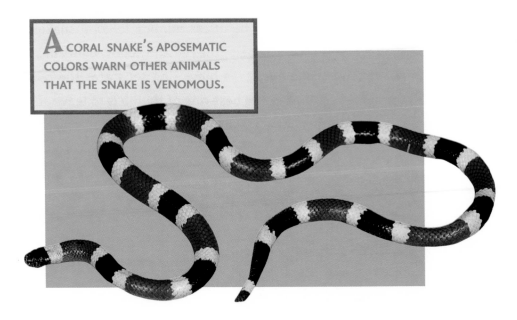

A CORAL SNAKE'S APOSEMATIC COLORS WARN OTHER ANIMALS THAT THE SNAKE IS VENOMOUS.

COPY CATS

Some warning colors have been so successful that other animals have evolved similar colors. For example, neither mountain king snakes nor milk snakes are venomous, yet they have colors that are very similar to the warning colors of coral snakes. Scientists have a special name for this kind of "copycatting." It is called *mimicry* (MI-mik-ree).

Mimicry allows nonvenomous and nonpoisonous animals to fool their enemies into leaving them alone—even though the mimics aren't dangerous. Reptiles aren't the only animal mimics. Mimicry has also evolved in insects, fishes, and other creatures.

By the way, there is an easy way to tell the difference between a venomous coral snake and its harmless mimics. In coral snakes, the red and yellow rings touch, just like the red and yellow lights in a traffic signal. In coral snake mimics, a black ring separates the red and yellow (or white) colors. But the best rule of thumb is to leave *all* wild animals alone, whether they appear safe or not.

THE CALIFORNIA MOUNTAIN KING SNAKE IS ONE OF MANY ANIMALS THAT GAINS PROTECTION BY MIMICKING VENOMOUS OR POISONOUS ANIMALS. IT LOOKS VERY SIMILAR TO THE CORAL SNAKE.

dull-colored sticks much more often than they attacked sticks that had been painted to look like coral snakes.

Aposematic coloring can also be found in a group of venomous snakes called sea snakes. More than 50 different kinds of sea snakes live in the Indian and Pacific oceans. Most live in the warm, shallow waters of coral reefs. One kind, the yellow-bellied sea snake, can also be found drifting far from shore, where it hunts small fish that gather just below the ocean's surface.

Sea snakes are some of the most venomous creatures on Earth. Their venom is far deadlier than the venom of coral snakes, rattlesnakes, or even king cobras. Sea snakes use their venom to kill the fish they eat and to defend themselves against predators. It's not necessarily a good thing, however, for a sea snake to use its venom to defend itself. Venom can take a lot of energy to make— energy that could be used for growing or hunting. Also, the more often a sea snake or other venomous animal is attacked, the more likely it is to get hurt—even if it can defend itself.

Like coral snakes, many sea snakes solve this problem by warning predators up front. For example, the yellow-bellied sea snake has bright, splashy colors that tell predators not to try anything. Over millions of years, predators have evolved to pay attention to this warning. Only a few

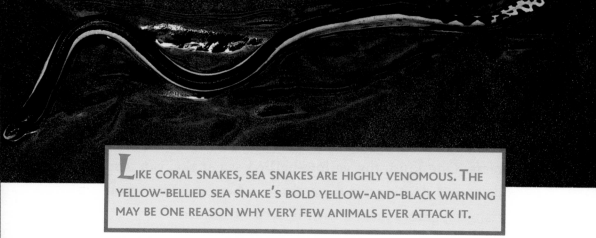

kinds of sharks and sea eagles dare attack sea snakes. This keeps sea snakes from constantly having to defend themselves and increases their chances of survival.

Lock-Jaw Lizards

Snakes are not the only reptiles that have evolved aposematic coloring. The Gila monster is one of only two kinds of venomous lizards in the world. (The other kind is the Mexican beaded lizard.) It lives in the deserts of the Southwest, primarily in Arizona and northern Mexico. Gila monsters spend most of their time hidden in cool underground burrows or under rocks and bushes. They emerge only to hunt, mate, or bask in the sun.

A GILA MONSTER'S ORANGE AND BLACK COLORS MAY SERVE AS A WARNING OR AS CAMOUFLAGE, DEPENDING ON THE SITUATION.

The Gila monster is an animal whose colors probably perform double-duty. From a distance, the animal's orange-and-black skin may actually act as camouflage in the sunburned desert lands where it lives. Up close, these same colors vividly spell "D-A-N-G-E-R!"

Unlike sea snakes, Gila monsters do not need their

venom to hunt. They feed on eggs and on slow-moving lizards, insects, baby birds, and rodents. Venom, however, is a valuable defense against hawks, coyotes, and other predators. When a Gila monster is threatened, it may lock its jaws onto its attacker and hold on for up to 15 minutes. During this time, venom runs up special grooves in the lizard's lower teeth and into the wound of the attacker. This venom isn't as potent as sea snake venom—few people have died from it—but it can make animals very sick. The striking skin of a Gila monster warns predators to keep their distance and helps prevent the Gila monster from having to bite its enemies.

Fantastic Frogs

Some of the most stunning aposematic colors can be found in a group of amphibians called poison-arrow, or poison-dart, frogs. There are about 100 different kinds of poison-arrow frogs, and they live in the tropical rain forests of Central and South America. Poison-arrow frogs are not venomous—they can't bite you and inject poison into you—but their skin contains deadly poisons.

Like other aposematic signals, the brightly colored

THE SKINS OF POISON-ARROW FROGS RANGE FROM FAIRLY DULL TO EXTREMELY BRIGHT. GENERALLY, FROGS WITH MORE POISONOUS SKIN ARE MORE BRIGHTLY COLORED.

skin of poison-arrow frogs warns predators to stay away. But people have found many uses for the frogs' deadly defense. In the past, Central American Indians have rubbed the frogs' poisons onto the tips of arrows or darts used for hunting. More recently, scientists have found

25

that the frogs' poisons contain many interesting chemicals. Some of these may be useful for making pain killers or other medicines. This doesn't mean you should ever touch or play with a poison-arrow frog. If the poison from the frog's skin is accidentally swallowed or comes into contact with your eyes or with open wounds, it can cause extreme pain and even death.

Reptile Relationships

Not all bright colors in reptiles and amphibians warn other animals that they are poisonous or venomous. Like birds, many male lizards display bright colors to communicate with each other. Competition for territory can be fierce among some male lizards and bright colors allow one male to tell others they're in for a fight if they venture closer. A male's bright colors also tell female lizards that he is ready and available to mate.

Unfortunately, the same colors that a lizard uses to communicate may also attract the attention of predators. Chameleons solve this problem by turning their bright colors on and off. Most of the time, chameleons adopt cryptic colors that help them blend in with their surroundings. But chameleons are extremely territorial. When another male chameleon approaches, these lizards "turn up" their colors by changing the shapes and sizes

CHROMATOPHORES IN THIS CHAMELEON'S SKIN ALLOW IT TO CHANGE ITS COLORS RAPIDLY AND DRAMATICALLY.

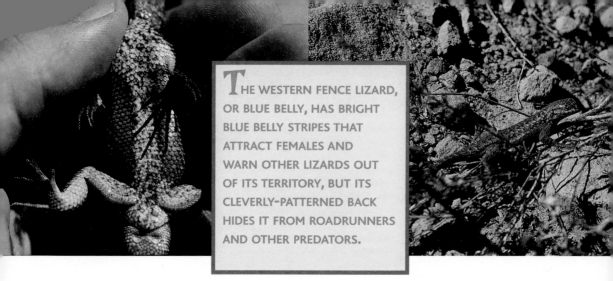

THE WESTERN FENCE LIZARD, OR BLUE BELLY, HAS BRIGHT BLUE BELLY STRIPES THAT ATTRACT FEMALES AND WARN OTHER LIZARDS OUT OF ITS TERRITORY, BUT ITS CLEVERLY-PATTERNED BACK HIDES IT FROM ROADRUNNERS AND OTHER PREDATORS.

of special skin cells called *chromatophores*. These cells contain colorful pigments that the chameleon exposes only when needed. Besides warning other males to stay away, male chameleons also "brighten up" when courting females.

Most lizards, however, cannot change color this dramatically and must solve the predator problem in other ways. The western fence, or blue belly, lizard has two bright blue stripes running down its sides. When the lizard rises up on its toes, female lizards and competing male lizards can clearly see these blue stripes. From above, however, all a hungry predator sees is the blue belly's camouflaged brown or gray back. By having camouflage on top and "dazzle" on the bottom, the blue belly gets the best of both worlds. It can send signals to other lizards *and* stay hidden from hunters.

three

Dazzling Insects

When most people think of dazzling insects, butter-flies flutter to mind first. Many butterflies are crypti-cally colored, but a surprising number dazzle and flash their way through our world. Butterflies display every color imaginable: red, blue, violet, green, orange, black, white, and colors in between. Some of these hues come from iridescence. Others burst from pigments in the tiny scales on the butterflies' wings.

Bright colors help butterflies identify members of their own species—an extremely useful feature during mating. Colors serve other purposes as well. Black and orange are especially common warning colors found in fritillaries, crescentspots, and monarchs. It's no surprise that these black-and-orange butterflies contain *alkaloids*

FOR MANY BUTTERFLIES, INCLUDING THE MONARCH AND THIS FRITILLARY, ORANGE-AND-BLACK COLORS WARN THAT THE ANIMALS ARE POISONOUS. SOME NONPOISONOUS BUTTERFLIES GAIN PROTECTION BY MIMICKING THESE SAME WARNING COLORS.

and other chemicals that make them taste bad to predators, such as birds. The butterflies obtain these chemicals by feeding on passionflowers and other plants that manufacture these poisons.

30

But not all black-and-orange butterflies taste bad. Like some snakes, butterflies can be mimics. Viceroy butterflies, for instance, look almost identical to toxic monarch butterflies. Unlike the monarchs, however, viceroys are perfectly edible. The viceroy's close resemblance to the monarch helps protect it from birds that have learned monarchs make a yucky meal.

Flash and Dazzle

Fritillaries, viceroys, and monarchs display their bright colors all the time, but other butterflies have evolved different approaches to coloration. Many butterflies have bright, shiny colors on the *dorsal*, or upper, sides of their wings, while their *ventral*, or bottom, sides are dark and cryptically colored. When the butterflies are at rest with their wings folded up, they are camouflaged against their surroundings. When they are flying, however, they are clearly visible to other animals. Entomologists, scientists who study insects, often refer to these butterflies as flash-and-dazzle butterflies.

For years, biologists have tried to figure out the value of the flash-and-dazzle lifestyle. Here's what they think: When a flash-and-dazzle butterfly is at rest, its cryptic underside hides the butterfly from predators. But if a bird or other predator happens to spot and attack the

THE SPECTACULAR BLUE MORPHO BUTTERFLY EMPLOYS A
FLASH-AND-DAZZLE SURVIVAL STRATEGY.

butterfly, the butterfly can take off and startle the predator with the flashing, bright upper surfaces of its wings. If the predator chases after the butterfly, the butterfly can again stop and disappear by folding up its wings. Scientists believe that this butterfly behavior often confuses predators and makes them lose track of their butterfly prey.

32

Like Caterpillar, Like Moth

Like their butterfly cousins, moths display a fantastic variety of colors. Most of these colors help camouflage the moths, but not all. The polka-dot wasp moth is commonly active during the day and displays bold black-and-white spotted wings and a shimmering blue abdomen with a red tip. The caterpillar of the polka-dot wasp moth is also vividly colored black and orange. If you guess that these colors are aposematic, you are right.

The caterpillar is called the oleander caterpillar, and it feeds on the poisonous leaves of oleanders. This gives it a chemical defense that keeps birds and ants from eating it. What's more, this chemical protection continues when the caterpillar *metamorphoses*, or changes, into the adult polka-dot wasp moth.

Many other caterpillars also contain chemical defenses. The caterpillars of monarch butterflies, for instance, feed on milkweed plants that give them chemical protection. Their multicolored stripes are a clear warning to stay away.

Some caterpillars, including the oleander caterpillar, also come equipped with bushy spines that break off

Poisonous moths and their caterpillars sometimes display warning colors. The polka-dot wasp moth and its caterpillar, the oleander caterpillar, are both active during the daytime. Their colors probably help keep predators away.

and stick into the skin of any animal that tastes or touches them. These spines often are loaded with poisons that leave a burning sensation on a hungry predator's tongue or skin.

Among the most amazing of these spiny caterpillars are the *processionary caterpillars.* These brightly colored creatures are often found marching end-to-end in search of food. Their marching ways give them several advantages. By marching end-to-end, the caterpillars appear bigger than they are and may intimidate hungry birds and other predators. Marching together also increases the size of their aposematic warning for predators to stay away.

MARCHING TOGETHER MAKES PROCESSIONARY CATERPILLARS APPEAR BIGGER THAN THEY ARE—AND INCREASES THE SIZE OF THEIR APOSEMATIC WARNING.

Brilliant Beetles

Beetles are the largest group of insects on Earth. Most beetles are cryptically colored, but some stand out. Many beetles have special glands, which secrete substances that repel other animals, and some of these beetles are aposematically colored. The metallic blue or green shells of some dung beetles, for instance, advertise that they taste bad. Not surprisingly, some "tasty" dung beetles gain protection by mimicking the colors of their bad-tasting relatives.

Among the most boldly colored beetles are the ladybird beetles. Many ladybird beetles are colored bright red and black or black and yellow. Unlike bad-tasting dung beetles, ladybird beetles do not have glands that secrete chemicals. Instead, the blood of ladybird beetles tastes bad. When threatened or attacked, the beetle leaks this blood through *pores*, or special openings, in its leg joints.

Ladybird beetles are not the only beetles that leak blood. A group of beetles called bloody-nosed beetles releases blood around their mouths when they are bothered or handled. These beetles are black, so again, the black-and-red combination of shell and blood warns predators to stay away. Alas, not all predators are both-

*L*ADYBIRD BEETLES ARE COLORFUL INSECTS THAT REPEL PREDATORS WITH THEIR BAD-TASTING BLOOD.

ered by warning colors or an insect's distasteful properties. Grizzly bears have been observed slurping up gallons of ladybird beetles that have gathered together to hibernate in the mountains.

Colorful Collections

Butterflies, moths, and beetles aren't the only insect dazzlers—not by a long shot! Almost every insect family contains members that sport dazzling colors. Bees and wasps are often colored black and yellow, a sign that they're dangerous. Some harmless fly mimics have evolved these same warning colors in the long-running battle to fool predators.

Grasshoppers, bugs, dragonflies, and many other kinds of insects also have colorful representatives. Many of these colorful creatures are poisonous or distasteful, but scientists still don't completely understand the advantages of being colorful for all of these insects.

The annual emergence of colorful insects can be especially dazzling in the tropics. During certain times of the year, large groups of brightly colored caterpillars, bugs, and other insects suddenly appear in tropical

MOST INSECT GROUPS HAVE COLORFUL REPRESENTATIVES. THIS MARDI-GRAS-COLORED GRASSHOPPER LIVES IN THE TROPICAL RAIN FORESTS OF MALAYSIA.

DURING CERTAIN TIMES OF THE YEAR, AN EXPLOSION OF COLORFUL INSECTS EMERGES IN THE TROPICS. THESE INSECT DAZZLERS WERE ALL FOUND WITHIN A 100-FOOT (31-M) AREA ON THE SAME DAY IN THE DRY TROPICAL FORESTS OF COSTA RICA.

forests. Scientists can never predict exactly when these events will occur. The timing probably depends on the weather and many other factors. But if you are lucky enough to be in the right place when the insects come out, you'll be treated to a display of insect "fireworks" you'll never forget.

41

THIS NUDIBRANCH AND THE ONE ON PAGE 4 OF THIS BOOK LIVE IN THE PACIFIC OCEAN, OFF THE COAST OF CALIFORNIA. NUDIBRANCHS ARE KNOWN FOR THEIR BRIGHT COLORS AND FOR STEALING POISONOUS NEMATOCYSTS FROM THE SEA ANEMONES THEY EAT.

four

Dazzling Fish
and Other Sea Creatures

The ocean is loaded with dazzlers of many shapes, kinds, and sizes. Like sea snakes, many brightly colored marine animals display aposematic colors. Some nudibranchs, or sea slugs, display spectacular colors that advertise they are poisonous. These poisons often come in the form of acids produced in a nudibranch's skin. Other nudibranchs are armed with little stinging cells called *nematocysts*. If another animal bothers one of these nudibranchs, the nematocysts fire, inflicting a painful surprise.

Bright colors are also used by marine animals for camouflage and display. Cephalopods—squids, octopuses, nautiluses, and cuttlefish—can change their colors almost instantaneously. The skin of cephalopods, like the skin of chameleons, is loaded with chromatophores, which rapidly change shape to produce different colors and designs. Cephalopods alter their colors to match their environment. The animals can quickly assume bright colors, however, when they are ready to mate or are warning other cephalopods to stay away.

Brilliant colors appear in many other marine animals besides nudibranchs and cephalopods. Of all the kinds of dazzling creatures in the ocean, however, one group out-dazzles all others—the fish.

Cold Water Show-Off

The vast majority of fish have evolved cryptic colors that camouflage them among their surroundings. This is especially true of fish in colder oceans. If you go diving along the Pacific coast of California, you may swim by hundreds of fish that look almost identical to the rocks, sand, and kelp. One exception is the garibaldi.

The adult garibaldi has an astonishing orange skin that is visible for long distances underwater. The question is, why would a fish want to advertise itself in a world full of animals looking for a fish dinner? The garibaldi is not poisonous or venomous, so what's going on?

THE GARIBALDI IS ONE OF THE FEW COLD-WATER MARINE
FISHES THAT HAS EVOLVED BRIGHT COLORS.

Garibaldis are territorial fish. Each one defends an area of rocks that provides it with food and a place to mate and raise its young. The fish's breathtaking bright-orange color probably sends a signal to other garibaldis: "This is my territory. Keep away from here!" This is not an idle threat. An adult garibaldi will aggressively attack any other adult garibaldis or predators that venture close. Interestingly, colors are also what protect young garibaldis from the aggressive adults. The young have blue stripes along their bodies, which evidently tell adult garibaldis that the "small fry" are not a threat.

Warm Water Wonders

Although the garibaldi stands out as one of the splashiest fish in the cool Pacific, it would hardly merit a yawn in the warm waters of the tropics.

The colorful fish of tropical coral reefs seem to defy explanation. Hundreds of species of tropical fish shimmer with bright—even shocking—colors. This overwhelming show of color has baffled biologists for years. They wonder, "How can so many fish call attention to themselves and not all get eaten?" As is often true in nature, there is no single answer to the question.

Some tropical fish colors are probably aposematic. Lionfish, for example, show off red and white stripes

WITH ITS CONTRASTING COLORS, THE LIONFISH OF THE TROPICS CLEARLY ADVERTISES ITS POISONOUS SPINES.

and multicolored "crowns," which are hard to miss underwater. It's not a warning to ignore because the lionfish's long, barbed dorsal spines are loaded with deadly poisons.

But what about the other colorful reef fish—the ones without poisons? Again, it depends on the fish. One highly visible fish is the cleaner wrasse. Cleaner wrasses are tiny black-and-white fish. Each one has a shimmering blue stripe along the top of its body. This fish has an important role on the reef. It sets up "cleaning stations" for other fish. The wrasses do a special dance to advertise to other fish that they are open and ready for business. The other fish respond to this dance by lining up to be cleaned.

With their small pincerlike teeth, cleaner wrasses pick algae and parasites off bigger fish. The bigger fish wait patiently and even open their mouths and gills so the cleaner wrasses can swim inside. In performing their cleaning duties, the wrasses get a free meal and probably improve the health of other reef fish.

THE TINY CLEANER WRASSE'S COLORFUL STRIPES AND UNDERWATER "DANCE," HELP FISH, SUCH AS THIS CORAL TROUT, IDENTIFY THE WRASSE.

48

In a world as complex and crowded as a coral reef, not all colors are what they seem. The sabre-toothed blenny is a small fish that mimics the cleaner wrasse almost exactly. When a fish comes up to be cleaned by a sabre-tooth blenny, the "customer" gets a nasty surprise. The blenny doesn't pick off parasites—it grabs a bite of skin or fin from the fish wanting to be cleaned!

Pretty Puzzles

Scientists can explain the colors of lionfish and cleaner wrasses fairly easily. The colors of these fish serve obvious functions and protect the fish from predators. The existence and role of color in hundreds of other reef fish is a greater mystery. Take the striking butterfly fishes. These common reef fishes are usually colored white, yellow, and black. They stand out prominently on the reef and would seem to make bright targets for predators. How can these fishes survive?

The answer may have to do with false eye spots. Butterfly fishes often have large black spots near their tails that resemble eyes. Many biologists believe that even though the butterfly fish is brightly colored, its eye spot fools predators and makes them attack the wrong end of the fish. Instead of fleeing in the direction the

BUTTERFLY FISH HAVE FALSE EYE SPOTS THAT MAY CONFUSE PREDATORS JUST LONG ENOUGH FOR THE FISH TO ESCAPE.

predator expects, the butterfly fish swims in the opposite direction and escapes unharmed.

The "eye-spot" theory seems reasonable, but not all biologists believe it. Some scientists doubt that predators are stupid enough to be fooled by fake eye spots for long. So how can dazzling reef fish, such as the butterfly fish, have such bright colors and still survive?

Colorful Conclusions

Biologists believe that the reason brightly colored fish survive on the coral reef and not in other places has to do with the actual construction of the reef. Coral reefs are built by living animals called *corals*. The corals come in many shapes and sizes and offer millions of hiding places for animals, including reef fish. If a predator comes along, a butterfly fish or other colorful fish can quickly dash into a hole or coral crevice until the coast is clear. Still, this doesn't explain why many reef fish *have* bright colors in the first place. The answer to that question may tie in with reef fishes' coldwater cousin, the garibaldi.

Like the garibaldi, many tropical reef fish are extremely territorial. They inhabit small patches of the reef and defend their territories against other fish, especially fish of the same species. Color probably serves two functions for these fish. First, it helps them identify others of their own kind. This is an especially important ability on a coral reef, where up to 2,000 different kinds of fish often live close together. Second, a fish's colors warn other fish of the same species to keep their distance or risk a fight.

Bright colors, however, serve one more role in certain fish social systems. Some of the most interesting fish on the coral reef, such as wrasses, live in "harems." In each harem, there is one dominant male or female and many subordinate adults and juveniles. In most cases, only the dominant fish mate. They take on the brightest, boldest colors, and the subordinate fish wear duller "outfits." A dominant fish's dazzling appearance not only warns intruding fish to stay out of its territory, but also firmly tells members of its own harem who is boss.

PEOPLE'S NATURAL COLORS ARE RATHER DRAB, BUT OUR
BRIGHT CLOTHES CAN HELP US COMMUNICATE WITH EACH OTHER
OR JUST MAKE US FEEL GOOD ABOUT OURSELVES.

five

The Color Kings

You've just had a look at many of nature's dazzling creatures and learned how their colors help them to survive. But many more colorful creatures share our planet than could find places in this book. Colorful spiders, worms, sponges, sea stars, and other animals live on Earth. And there's one more group of colorful creatures that may be the most dazzling of all—us.

Although peoples' natural skin and hair colors are usually fairly dull, we make ourselves dazzling in other ways—with our clothes, make-up, hairstyles, and even the flashy cars we drive. In fact, humans often spend more money on their appearances than on food! Sometimes, we dazzle up to help us feel happy or good about ourselves. But like other animals, we use colors to communicate with each other, too. Dark colors can tell other people that we are serious or sad. Bright colors may help us attract friends or mates.

The next time you pick out which clothes to wear, think about how *you* use colors to communicate. Then observe the birds, insects, and other animals around you. You may realize that you and other animal dazzlers aren't so different after all.

resources

Books

Anderson, L. W. *Light & Color*. Austin, TX: Raintree/Steck-Vaughn, 1987.

Collard, Sneed B., III. *Sea Snakes*. Honesdale, PA: Boyds Mill Press, 1993.

———. *Smart Survivors*. Minoqua, WI: NorthWord, 1994.

Crump, Donald R. *Secrets of Animal Survival*. Washington, DC: National Geographic, 1983.

Martin, James. *Hiding Out: Camouflage in the Wild*. New York: Crown, 1993.

Patent, Dorothy Hinshaw. *Animals Black and White*. New York: Walker, 1998.

Perry, Phyllis J. *Hide and Seek: Creatures in Camouflage*. Danbury, CT: Franklin Watts, 1997.

Internet

The Chameleon Research Center's home page provides lots of information about chameleons.
http://www.concentric.net/~Mglavin/index.html

A collaborative effort of the Nebraska Game and Parks Commission and teachers and students at Fredstrom Elementary School in Lincoln, Nebraska, this site updates the student's three-year project collecting data on monarch butterflies.
http://ngp.ngpc.state.ne.us/monarch/monarch.html

Check out Jeff's Nudibranch Page, which has lots of color photos of nudibranches.
http://home.mem.net/~zipper/crinoids.htm

Sponsored by the University of Nevada, this web site provides information on Gila monsters.
http://hrcweb.lv-hrc.nevada.edu/mbm/reptiles/gila-text.htm

This site features information on poison arrow frogs.
http://206.1.0.131/index.html

glossary

Alkaloids   a large group of chemicals that are poisonous or bad-tasting to most animals

Aposematic coloring   colors or markings on an animal that warn other animals it is venomous, poisonous, or dangerous in some other way

Camouflage   colors or other features of an animal that help it blend in with the habitat in which it lives

Carotenoids   pigments that are responsible for many reds, oranges, and yellows in animals

Chromatophores   pigment-containing cells found in the skins and shells of many animals

Corals   ocean animals that often live together in large colonies; most have hard skeletons that, over many years, produce large structures called reefs

Cryptic coloration   colors that make an animal difficult to see against its background

Dorsal   the top or upper surface of an animal

Iridescence   color produced by separating, blocking, and shifting sunlight of different wavelengths

Iris   the colored portion of the eye; the pupil in the center of the iris controls how much light enters the eye

Melanins   pigments that produce browns and blacks, and some reds and yellows, in animals

Metamorphosis   the transformation from the larval to the adult form that occurs in many invertebrates and amphibians; for example, a caterpillar forming a chrysalis and metamorphosing into a butterfly

Mimicry   the existence of animals that have evolved to resemble other species of animals or plants

Nematocyst   a type of stinging cell found in many animals; they are used for defense

Pigments   chemicals or proteins that produce color; they are found in the skin, fur, feathers, and scales of many animals

Pores   tiny openings in an animal's skin or shell that allow liquids and gases to pass through

Predator   an animal that hunts and eats other animals

Prey   an animal that is hunted and eaten by a *predator*

Processionary caterpillars   caterpillars that often march end-to-end in a line as they search for food or shelter

Pterins   pigments that, like *carotenoids*, are responsible for many reds, oranges, and yellows in animals.

Synthesize   to make from basic ingredients; the bodies of animals can synthesize color-producing *pigments*

Tropical cloud forest   a type of forest located in the mountains of tropical countries where trade winds produce an almost constant blanket of clouds

Tyndall scattering   a process by which light is scattered by feathers or skin to produce a blue or green color

Ventral   the lower or bottom surface of an animal

index

Sneed B. Collard III is the author of 15 award-winning science and nature books for young people. His two previous Franklin Watts titles, *Monteverde: Science and Scientists in a Costa Rican Cloud Forest* (1997) and *Alien Invaders: The Continuing Threat of Exotic Species* (1996), received the highest possible recommendations from *Booklist* and *Science Books and Films*. His other books include *Sea Snakes, Animal Dads, Our Wet World*, and *Creepy Creatures*.

Each year, Mr. Collard travels widely, speaking to thousands of students and teachers throughout the United States. When he is not writing or speaking, he enjoys hiking, kayaking, and bird-watching near his home in Missoula, Montana.